D0504484

Animal Neighbours

Snake

Stephen Savage

HODDER
Wayland

An imprint of Hodder Children's Books

Animal Neighbours

Titles in this series:

**Badger • Bat • Blackbird • Deer • Duck • Fox
Hare • Hedgehog • Mole • Mouse • Otter • Owl
Rat • Snake • Swallow • Toad**

**For more information on this series and other Hodder Wayland titles,
go to www.hodderwayland.co.uk**

Conceived and produced for Hodder Wayland by

Nutshell
MEDIA

Intergen House, 65–67 Western Road, Hove BN3 2JQ, UK
www.nutshellmedialtd.co.uk

Commissioning Editor: Vicky Brooker
Editor: Polly Goodman
Designer: Mayer Media Ltd
Illustrator: Jackie Harland

Published in Great Britain in 2005 by Hodder Wayland, an imprint of Hodder Children's Books.

British Library Cataloguing in Publication Data
Savage, Stephen
Snake. – (Animal neighbours)
1. Snakes – Juvenile literature
I. Title
597.9'6

ISBN 0 7502 4663 4

Cover: A grass snake tastes the air with its tongue as it hunts for food.
Title page: A grass snake climbs the lower branches of a willow tree.

Picture acknowledgements
FLPA *Title page*, 8, 12 (Derek Middleton), 14 (W. Rohdich), 17 (Roger Wilmshurst), 26 (Tony Hamblin), 28 top (Derek Middleton); naturepl.com 7 (John Downer), 15 (Chris Packham), 19 (Artur Tabor), 24 (Dietmar Nill), 25 (Tony Phelps); NHPA *Cover* (Stephen Dalton), 6 (Daryl Balfour), 13 (Michael Leach), 22, 23, 28 left (Hellio & Van Ingen); OSF 9, 10 (Tony Allen), 11 (Ian West), 16 (Mark Hamblin), 20, 21 (Paulo de Oliveira), 27 (Philippe Henry), 28 right, 28 bottom (Tony Allen).

Printed and bound in China.

Hodder Children's Books
A division of Hodder Headline Limited
338 Euston Road, London NW1 3BH

Contents

Meet the Snake

Snakes are long, legless reptiles. There are about 2,900 species in the world today. They live on all the continents except Antarctica, but only on some islands. Snakes have adapted to living in many different habitats, including rainforests, grasslands, woodlands, mountains and deserts. One group even lives in the sea.

This book is about the grass snake, Europe's largest and most common species.

▲ **The red part of this map shows where grass snakes live in the world today.**

Skin

The scales are covered by a thin layer of skin, which is shed up to three times a year.

Body

Grass snakes are usually a grey-green colour, although occasionally they are black. Their colour provides perfect camouflage against their surroundings. The heart, liver and other internal organs are protected by a rib cage that runs the whole length of the body.

Tail

The tail can coil around and grip objects, which can help the snake to climb.

4

Eyes

The eyes are on the sides of the head, which helps the snake spot the movement of prey and predators all around it. Snakes have no eyelids. Instead, each eye is covered by a protective, transparent scale.

▼ **A grass snake.**

Nostrils

Two nostrils positioned on the end of the snout allow the snake to swim with just the top of its head above water to breathe.

Mouth

Small teeth inside the mouth are used to grip prey. The snake cannot chew. Instead, it swallows prey whole, dislocating its lower jawbones to swallow large prey.

Tongue

Snakes have a narrow, forked tongue. As it is flicked in and out, it collects scents from the surroundings and helps the snake find prey.

Neck

The grass snake has distinctive dark marks on either side of its head and neck.

Scales

Dry, shiny scales protect the body and prevent water loss. Much larger scales on the underside of the body grip the ground, helping the snake to move or climb.

◀ **This shows the size of a grass snake compared to a domestic cat.**

SNAKE FACTS

The grass snake's scientific name is *Natrix natrix*, which comes from the Latin word *natrix* meaning 'water snake'.

Another name for the grass snake is the ringed snake, because of the dark marks on either side of its head and neck.

Male grass snakes are 70–82 cm long. Females are larger, about 93–110 cm long, although the longest recorded female measured 200 cm.

The Snake Family

Snakes belong to a group of cold-blooded animals known as reptiles, which include lizards, turtles, tortoises and crocodiles. Most snakes live on the ground, but some, such as the tropical thread snake, spend most of the time in underground burrows. Others, such as the African boomslang snake, live in trees. A few snakes even live in the sea.

All snakes are predators, but they have developed different techniques of killing their prey. Large snakes, such as the reticulated python from Southeast Asia, kill their prey by wrapping their body around their victim and squeezing until the animal suffocates.

▼ This rock python in Africa has squeezed a hare to death and is swallowing it whole.

▲ The Mozambique spitting cobra can spray poison from its fangs into the eyes of an enemy up to 3 metres away.

Other snakes kill using poison. The Indian cobra and other poisonous snakes kill their prey with a poisonous bite. The poison is injected from two large fangs that hang from the roof of their mouth.

Snakes defend themselves from predators in different ways. The grass snake and many other species are a similar colour to their surroundings, so they use camouflage to hide from their enemies. Others take more dramatic action. If disturbed, cobras rear upright and spread out the scales either side of their neck to scare off an enemy.

BIGGEST AND SMALLEST

The longest snakes are the reticulated python and the anaconda, which can both grow up to 10 m long. The heaviest snake is the anaconda, which can weigh up to 250 kg. The longest poisonous snake is the king cobra, which can reach 5.5 m in length. The smallest snake is the Martinique thread snake from the Caribbean, which grows to a length of just 10.8 cm.

Birth and Growing Up

It is early summer, and a female grass snake finds a nest site to lay her eggs. She looks for somewhere that is warm and hidden from predators. Favourite places are compost heaps, where the rotting waste gives off warmth as it decomposes. Other nest sites include manure heaps, dunghills, haystacks, old tree trunks, rotting reeds, ploughed fields and piles of leaves.

▼ A female grass snake prepares to leave her newly laid eggs.

EGGS

Grass snake eggs are white, with a soft, leathery shell. They are about 15 mm wide and 25 mm long.

As the snake grows inside, the egg expands. So although some eggs are oval-shaped, others become long and bumpy.

Snakes lay between 10–40 eggs, depending on their age. Young snakes may lay up to 10, whereas older snakes may lay up to 40 eggs.

A group of eggs is called a clutch.

The female slowly lays her eggs, one at a time. It may take several days before they have all been laid. Once the last one has been laid, the female abandons the eggs and provides no further care.

If the eggs have been laid in a location that is warm enough, such as a compost heap, the eggs will hatch about five weeks later. In cooler locations, they may take two months or more to hatch, and some may not hatch at all.

Inside each egg, the young snake, called a snakelet, develops into a miniature version of the adult. Each snakelet has an egg tooth on its snout, which it uses to slash holes in the eggshell. Once the hole is big enough, the snakelet sticks its head out and tastes the air with its tongue.

▶ A hatching grass snake tastes the air with its tongue. Sometimes snakelets do not completely leave the egg for a few hours.

Early days

All the snakelets hatch at about the same time, which may take several hours. The newly hatched snakelets are often darker skinned than the adults. Measuring only 15–18 centimetres long, they can see and move around immediately, and are independent straight away. The egg tooth drops off within 12 hours after hatching since it will no longer be needed.

Within hours of hatching, the snakelets leave the nest chamber and explore the rest of the nest site. They find and eat their first food, including insects and young slugs and worms.

▲ This newly hatched grass snake glides over the other eggs as it explores the nest chamber.

SHEDDING SKIN

As snakelets grow, they shed the outer layer of their skin. This is called sloughing. A special fluid is produced between the living and dead layers of skin, which separates and softens the layers. The snake rubs its snout against something rough until the skin around its head starts to peel. Then it literally crawls out of its skin, which usually comes away in one piece, turned inside out. Adult snakes only slough once a year, but young snakes may do so three times a year as they continually outgrow their skin.

Within a few days they leave the nest site and spread out into the surrounding area. Little bigger than large worms, the young snakes are a perfect sized meal for various mammals and birds, and many are killed and eaten in these early days.

▼ A snake has crawled out of this colourless, almost transparent skin, leaving it in one piece.

Habitat

Grass snakes like damp habitats. Their homes include riverbanks, ponds and ditches. However, they also live in dry habitats such as woodlands, grasslands and heathlands, often with boggy areas nearby. They also live on farmland, in hedgerows and in urban habitats, as long as there is dense vegetation to hide beneath.

Grass snakes often move from one habitat to another in the summer, when they are looking for food. Some stay in one feeding area, while others will travel up to 4 kilometres in search of food, before returning to the place where they will hibernate in the autumn.

▲ This grass snake is climbing in the low branches of a willow tree. It coils its tail and body around the branches to stop it falling off.

COLD-BLOODED

Unlike warm-blooded animals such as mammals, which control their body temperature using food, snakes are cold-blooded. This means their body temperature changes with the temperature of their surroundings and they rely on the sun to give them heat. Snakes will die if they get too hot or too cold, so they will bask in sunshine to warm themselves up, but if they get too hot, they move from the sun to the shade to cool down.

Grass snakes are mainly active during the day because they need to use the heat of the sun to warm their bodies (see box). They regularly bask in sunlit areas and, although they live alone for most of the time, a number of snakes can be found basking side by side. Occasionally, a grass snake can be seen basking on a garden path or patio.

▼ A grass snake basks on a large rock that has been warmed by the sun's heat.

Water and swimming

In the summer months, grass snakes are found mainly in or near water, where they can feed on frogs and other amphibians, their favourite food. They look for secluded places that have little human disturbance, with plants at the water's edge. These habitats provide good hunting sites as well as places to hide from predators. Watery habitats include ponds, marshes, canals and ditches on farmland.

▲ A frog is taken by surprise as a grass snake's head appears out of the mud on a pond's edge.

▲ A grass snake swims through pondweed.

SEA SNAKES

Grass snakes are just one of several species of snake that can swim. Sea snakes live for most or all of their lives at sea. They live in tropical regions of the world and are found in coastal waters, mangrove swamps and coral reefs. Sea snakes eat fish, which they kill with a poisonous bite. Some species lay eggs, while others produce live young born in the sea. The sea snake's tail is a flat shape, which provides extra water resistance, helping it to swim.

Grass snakes are excellent swimmers. They swim using a side-to-side movement, often with just their head held above the surface. Snakes swim slowly when hunting, or quickly if crossing a pond. Their air-filled lungs help them to float. Snakes also dive when hunting, often staying underwater for 15–30 minutes. If they are chased into the water by a predator, grass snakes can hold their breath and remain submerged for over an hour.

Hibernation

The winter months are not warm enough for grass snakes to survive out in the open, so during the winter, they enter a special type of sleep, called hibernation. Towards the end of the summer, they eat plenty of food. They need to build up enough fat reserves to last them throughout the winter months, when they will not be eating.

In the autumn, grass snakes start travelling towards hibernation sites. These might be underground places such as disused fox or badger holes, or the crevices of walls or garden compost heaps. The snakes may need to travel some distance to find suitable hibernation sites and some adults will return to the same sites they used the previous year. If there is a shortage of suitable sites, several grass snakes will hibernate together.

▲ A grass snake emerges from hibernation. It has spent the cold winter behind gravestones in an overgrown corner of a churchyard.

16

MOVEMENT

Grass snakes have two main ways of moving. They can wriggle their body from side to side in S-shaped curves. They can also move straight forwards by gripping the ground with the scales on their belly. This method of moving is also used to climb up into bushes, small trees and hedgerows.

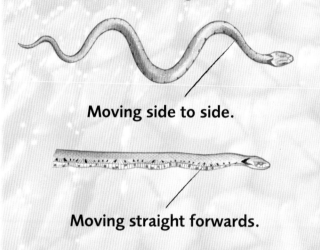

Moving side to side.

Moving straight forwards.

Larger, older snakes usually hibernate first, possibly because they already have enough fat reserves built up to live off during hibernation. Smaller, younger snakes start to hibernate a few weeks later.

The length of time grass snakes hibernate will depend on the weather, but it usually lasts from October until April. In colder winters they will hibernate for longer. In warmer winters they will wake up earlier.

▼ A grass snake peers out from its hibernation site beneath a fallen branch.

Food

Grass snakes are carnivores. They eat a variety of small animals, both on land and in water. On land, their prey includes toads, lizards and sometimes even small mammals such as mice and voles. They occasionally raid birds' nests and eat the eggs or chicks. When food is scarce they may also eat small invertebrates such as worms and beetles.

▼ The grass snake is in the centre of its food chain.

Snake food chain

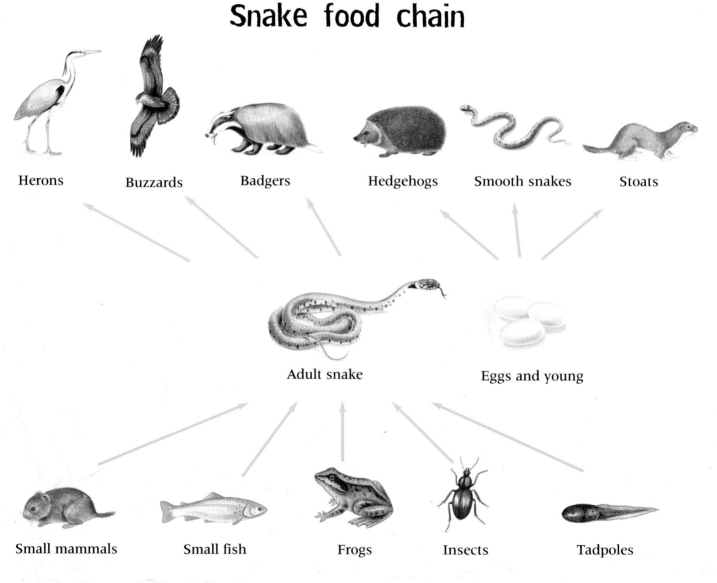

Herons   Buzzards   Badgers   Hedgehogs   Smooth snakes   Stoats

Adult snake   Eggs and young

Small mammals   Small fish   Frogs   Insects   Tadpoles

The illustrations are not to scale.

In water, grass snakes catch and eat tadpoles, small fish and newts. Young grass snakes mainly eat frog and toad tadpoles in water and small invertebrates on land.

Like many predators, grass snakes prefer to eat a large meal, such as a frog, rather than several small ones, which would use up more energy. To eat large prey, the snake grasps it by its head. It then moves each side of its jaws forward, one at a time, to ease its victim into its mouth and down its throat. Snakes can produce large amounts of saliva to help them swallow prey. They can also painlessly dislocate their lower jawbones if necessary.

DRINKING

Grass snakes need to drink water, usually from a pond, stream or puddle. They can also suck up dew or raindrops that have settled on grass through the tongue groove in their lip.

▼ A grass snake dislocates its lower jaw so it can swallow a large frog.

Hunting

▲ A grass snake's lunge is too quick for an unwary frog.

Grass snakes are active hunters, slithering through grass or gliding through water in search of prey. They use both smell and sight to hunt. As the snake's tongue is flicked in and out it collects scents left by passing prey. The snake follows a scent in the direction that it is strongest.

Having followed the scent of its prey, the grass snake locates it using its eyes. The snake glides silently along the ground to get close to its victim without it noticing. Then, at the last moment, it lunges forward and grabs the prey with its mouth. Small, grasping teeth hold on to the struggling prey, which is swallowed alive and whole.

After feeding, snakes often lie in the sun. The warmth raises their body temperature, which speeds up the process of digestion. It may take several days to digest a large meal, so snakes often hide away and rest somewhere quiet until they are hungry again. When they are not hibernating, grass snakes can survive without food for a week if they remain still, since resting uses up very little energy.

JACOBSON'S ORGAN

The Jacobson's organ, along with the nostrils, gives the snake a good sense of smell. Positioned in the roof of the mouth, it contains lots of nerve endings, which are very sensitive to smell. As the snake flicks its tongue out it picks up scent particles. When the tongue is pulled back in, the particles are passed to the Jacobson's organ, which passes information about the scent to the brain.

Snakes rely on their eyesight to ▶ find and catch prey underwater.

Finding a Mate

Grass snakes are ready to mate when they are 5 years old. Around April time, when the air and ground is warmed by spring sunshine, they come out of hibernation. Before they look for a mate they must eat, so they bask in sunny places to warm their bodies and then hunt for food.

▼ Two male grass snakes chase a female in an attempt to mate.

NEST SITES

Although the female grass snake provides no care for her eggs or young, she will travel long distances to find a suitable nest site, where her eggs will be safe and develop properly. Natural nest sites are hard to find, so although snakes live alone for most of the year, several females often nest together.

▲ A male grass snake twists his body around the larger female as he prepares to mate.

Mating usually takes place during a period of sunny weather, when snakes are most active. Sometimes it takes place within a few days after they have come out of hibernation, near the hibernation site. At other times mating takes place later, in May or June, when the snakes have dispersed to their summer feeding areas.

A male courts a female snake by rubbing his chin and head along her back. The pair may also lie side by side, twisting their bodies around each other. After mating, the male will leave the female, who may mate with one or two other males. About eight weeks after mating, the female finds a safe, warm place and lays

Threats

Grass snakes can live for up to 20 years, but most live to the age of 9. They are eaten by many different predators, including both mammals and birds. On land, grass snakes have little defence against the sharp claws and teeth of a badger or fox, and they provide tasty meals for buzzards and other birds of prey. They are plucked from water by the stabbing beaks of herons or the teeth of stoats.

▼ **Foxes prey on a wide range of animals, including grass snakes.**

▲ This grass snake is pretending to be dead so that a predator will not eat it.

EGGS AND SNAKELETS

Snakelets are eaten by hedgehogs, smooth snakes, blackbirds and fish. The eggs are eaten by rats and stoats, which raid the nests. The most dangerous time for young snakes is during their first hibernation. Many do not find enough food before they hibernate and die of starvation. Others do not burrow deep enough into the hibernation den, and freeze to death during cold weather.

To defend themselves from predators, grass snakes rely mainly on their bodies' camouflage and speed. Sometimes they try to fool their attacker. A cornered grass snake may hiss or dart forwards as it pretends to be a poisonous snake about to attack. If attacked, grass snakes can produce a foul-smelling liquid from their anal glands. As a last resort they may pretend to be dead, since most predators prefer live prey.

People and snakes

Many of the grass snake's natural habitats, such as wetlands, grasslands and heathlands, have been destroyed over the past 50 years by new building developments. The drainage of wetland areas has been disastrous for grass snakes. When these are drained, the snake's amphibian prey disappears. Although mice often move into drained wetlands, they are only a small part of the snake's diet. Mice are also mainly nocturnal, whereas snakes are active during the day.

▼ This wetland is being filled in to build a new road.

▲ When garden waste is burned, grass snakes and other wildlife hiding beneath can be killed.

LOVE OR HATE?

Many people are afraid of snakes, even though only a few European species are harmful. Some people fear them because of the way they move and have 'staring', unblinking eyes. For some Christians, snakes represent evil because the Bible associates them with the devil. But not everyone hates snakes. Thousands of people around the world keep certain species as pets. When raised in captivity from birth, boa constrictors have a gentle nature and can be safely handled.

As their natural habitat has been destroyed, grass snakes have moved into gardens, parks and allotments. However, even gardens can be dangerous places. Unaware of a snake's nest, a gardener may accidentally destroy the eggs by digging up a compost heap.

Some people kill grass snakes because they think they are dangerous, but they are harmless to humans. In Britain and many other European countries, grass snakes are protected by law and it is illegal to kill, injure or sell them.

Snake Life Cycle

1 Grass snake eggs are laid in June or July, in a compost heap or other warm, humid nest site.

2 After five weeks, the eggs hatch. The snakelets are 15–18 cm long and can see and move straight away.

3 When they are only a few days old, the snakelets leave the nest site and move to summer feeding areas.

4 In the autumn, the young snakes travel in search of hibernation sites.

5 When they are 5 years old, grass snakes are ready to mate.

Snake Clues

Look for the following clues to help you find a grass snake. If you see a snake, always watch it from a safe distance just in case it is a dangerous species. If you stay still, you will be able to watch it for longer before it notices you and slithers away.

Basking
On sunny days, look for grass snakes basking in the sun on garden paths or patios, in fields, heathland or woodland.

Ponds, rivers and ditches
Look out for grass snakes in or near water, especially ponds, rivers or ditches where there are frogs and other amphibians. When a grass snake is swimming, you can just see its head above water and a V-shaped track left behind it in the water.

Compost heaps
Look for snakes beneath compost heaps in gardens or allotments. Use a long stick to probe inside. If you see a snake, be careful not to disturb it.

Eggshells
Empty snake eggshells may be found in a compost heap. They are white and paper-thin with a leathery feel.

Skin
You might find the remains of a grass snake's skin, either in one piece or in smaller pieces. The skin is colourless and almost transparent.

Grass snake, adder or slow worm?
Grass snakes look quite similar to adders and slow worms. You can tell the difference by looking at the colour, size and eyes of each animal (see below).

Grass snake
Grey-green colour, with a dark band around the neck. Round pupils.

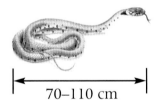

70–110 cm

Adder
Grey or brown colour with a zigzag pattern down their back. Slit-shaped pupils. Adders are poisonous snakes.

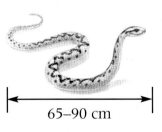

65–90 cm

Slow worm
Grey, light-brown or bronze. Females have a black stripe along their back. Eyelids that close. Slow worms are legless lizards, not snakes.

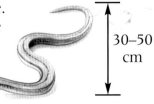

30–50 cm

Glossary

amphibians A group of animals such as toads, frogs and newts that usually live on land but return to water to lay their eggs.

camouflage The colour or pattern of some animals that helps them to blend in with their surroundings and makes them hard to see.

carnivores Animals that eat mainly other animals.

clutch A number of eggs laid at one time by the same female.

cold-blooded An animal whose body temperature is the same as its surroundings. It warms its body by lying in sunlight and cools down by moving to the shade.

compost heap Grass cuttings, vegetable peel and other plant matter that is allowed to decay to make natural fertiliser.

court Animal behaviour that is used to attract a mate, such as a dance or call.

decompose To break down, decay and rot.

dislocate To move out of a normal position.

dunghills Piles of animal droppings.

habitat The area where an animal or plant naturally lives.

hatch To come out from an egg.

hibernation When an animal spends the winter asleep, usually in a hole or den. Some toads, bats and snakes hibernate.

humid Slightly wet, moist or damp.

invertebrates Small animals without a backbone. Worms, slugs and insects are all invertebrates.

predator An animal that eats other animals.

prey Animals that are killed and eaten by predators.

reptiles A group of animals including snakes and lizards, that are cold-blooded with scaly skin.

sloughing To shed a dead outer layer of skin.

smooth snake A European species of snake that kills by constriction.

snakelets Young snakes.

tadpoles Young amphibians before they have grown legs.

tropical regions Areas of the world where it is hot most of the time.

vegetation Plants that provide shelter or food for animals.

wetlands A marshy area of land.

Finding Out More

Other books to read

Animal Classification by Polly Goodman (Hodder Wayland, 2004)

Animal Young: Reptiles by Rod Theodorou (Heinemann, 1999)

Circle of Life: Pond Life by David Stewart (Watts, 2002)

Classifying Living Things: Classifying Reptiles by Andrew Solway (Heinemann, 2003)

Food Chains and Webs: River Food Chains; Grassland Food Chains by Emma Lynch (Heinemann, 2004)

From Egg to Adult: The Life Cycle of Reptiles by Mike Unwin (Heinemann, 2004)

How Things Grow: From Tadpole to Frog by Sally Morgan (Chrysalis, 2003)

Life Cycles: Frogs and other Amphibians by Sally Morgan (Chrysalis, 2001)

Life Cycles: From Tadpole to Frog by Gerard Legg and David Stewart (Watts, 1998)

Living Nature: Amphibian by Angela Royston (Chrysalis, 2002)

Microhabitats: Life in a Pond by Clare Oliver (Evans, 2002)

What's the Difference?: Reptiles by Stephen Savage (Hodder Wayland, 2002)

Wild Britain: Parks and Gardens; Ponds; Meadows by R. & L. Spilsbury (Heinemann, 2003)

Wild Habitats of the British Isles: Rivers and Waterways; Towns and Cities by R. & L. Spilsbury (Heinemann, 2005)

Organisations to contact

Countryside Foundation for Education
PO Box 8, Hebden Bridge HX7 5YJ
www.countrysidefoundation.org.uk
An organisation that produces training and teaching materials to help the understanding of the countryside and its problems.

English Nature
Northminster House, Peterborough, Cambridgeshire PE1 1UA
www.englishnature.org.uk
A government body that promotes the conservation of English wildlife and the natural environment.

RSPB
The Lodge, Sandy, Bedfordshire SG19 2DL
www.rspb.org.uk
A wild birds conservation charity with wildlife reserves and a website that includes an A-Z of UK birds, news, surveys and webcams about issues concerning wild birds.

Wildlife Watch
National Office, The Kiln, Waterside, Mather Road, Newark, Nottinghamshire NG24 1WT
www.wildlifetrusts.org
The junior branch of the Wildlife Trusts, a network of local Wildlife Trusts caring for nearly 2,500 nature reserves, from rugged coastline to urban wildlife havens, protecting a huge number of habitats and species.

Index

Page numbers in **bold** refer to a photograph or illustration.